Your Complete Astrocartography Interpreter

Enables You To Read and Interpret

an Astrocartography Chart

also Known as a Astro-Relocation Map

BODHI BABA

DORRANCE
PUBLISHING CO
EST. 1920
PITTSBURGH, PENNSYLVANIA 15238

The contents of this work, including, but not limited to, the accuracy of events, people, and places depicted; opinions expressed; permission to use previously published materials included; and any advice given or actions advocated are solely the responsibility of the author, who assumes all liability for said work and indemnifies the publisher against any claims stemming from publication of the work.

All Rights Reserved
Copyright © 2022 by Bodhi Baba

No part of this book may be reproduced or transmitted, downloaded, distributed, reverse engineered, or stored in or introduced into any information storage and retrieval system, in any form or by any means, including photocopying and recording, whether electronic or mechanical, now known or hereinafter invented without permission in writing from the publisher.

Dorrance Publishing Co
585 Alpha Drive
Pittsburgh, PA 15238
Visit our website at *www.dorrancebookstore.com*

ISBN: 978-1-6376-4036-4
eISBN: 978-1-6376-4883-4

Dedication

This book is dedicated to my life-long friend and Guru Brother, Danny Kahalas. Who was like many of us, disciples of Baba Muktananda, who was more affectionately known as 'Gilly Gilly.' He passed away on 26 November 2018 at about 4:30 pm of an apparent stroke; the date I completed this book. We both shared an intense interest in Astrology, Yoga, Meditation, and other spiritual subjects. He will be greatly missed by all of us.

Foreword

IT IS WIDELY KNOWN THAT ASTROLOGY can assist and inform on different areas of life. Not only can it tell you your compatibility, it can advise you on upcoming events and future trends. This is easily achieved using different methods of predictive astrology, such as; short- and long-term transits, secondary, primary and additional types of progressions, solar, lunar and other sorts of return charts. Your birth chart helps in you gaining a better understanding of yourself by analysing the data it provides.

A birth chart enables us to probe into our past, highlighting prominent events which would have a significant effect on the fundamental shaping of our personalities. For example, when I had my first astrology chart interpretation, I was about twenty years old. The astrologer looked into my past and saw that around five years of age I had a near death experience. He stated it would have a profound positive or negative effect on my nature for the remainder of my life. As it turned out, even though I had tried hard to put that experience out of my mind, I nearly drowned on my fifth birthday when I fell out of a speeding motor boat in the middle of a lake. However, because my astrologer spotted that in my previous astrological influences, I was able to go back and process this experience the information enabled me to change something that could have had quite a harmful effect on me into something helpful & constructive at the time I was astonished that he was able to access all this information about me without knowing anything other than my date, time and place of birth. Now that I'm an astrologer understanding the craft, it comes as no surprise that I was able for example, to predict months beforehand the exact date of my teacher/Guru's death Swami Muktananda. More recently also able to foresee the election of Donald Trump as president when everyone else was expecting the opposite. Astrologers can forecast dates of conception, falling in love, reaching your career peaks and troughs, sickness, health, marriages, divorces and many more important life events, utilizing an accurate birth chart.

Hence, considering all above, we still need to touch upon *space*. Astrologers can tell you in linear *time* when something will either in the future occur or in the past has happened but what about *space*? Now I don't mean space like out there in the heavens but space in relation to the inhabitable surface of the Earth. This is where your astrocartogoraphy or relocation map comes into the picture and especially if you choose to relocate or move around the planet as many people are starting to do more and more these days. Therefore, using Astrocartogoraphy, we can determine by residing in a specific location the exact effect that place will have on you. This is why with two people who move to the same location, one person will love it there, while the other hates it. For example, I knew of a man who had existed miserably in one city all his life. Then when he was 29 years old and had finally had enough of this place, he moved to a new location that according to his astrocartogoraphy map was far superior to where he had lived before and his portrayal to me about the difference, he experienced between the two places was, "I feel like I've gone form living in a dungeon, into an enchanted forest."

The relatively unknown astrocartogoraphy chart is basically an extension of 'the relocation chart' which gives you the effects a place on the planet will have on you while you are there. However, your relocation map or astrocartography chart shows all locations at once. It expands these various influences all over the one globe for you to see all at once; good and bad, lucky and unlucky, successful and unsuccessful, comfortable and uncomfortable. And last but not least, it's not only useful for finding the optimum place for you to reside, should you choose to live there, but it can also show you where and where not to go for other reasons such as; your career, making money, romance, vacation, adventure, business, negotiations, education.

Now it's possible with a print out of your astrocartography map and this booklet to be your own astrologer. All you have to do is find the line or lines running over your existing or desired location, see what line(s) that is and then read the description that line would have on you while there. So, put simply, you can use the analysis given here in this book to determine what the effects of your present or any future location will be. If you do not already have a copy of your astrocartography chart you should contact me at; budbarber@hotmail.com and I'll mail it to you so you can begin your research and relocation and travel adventures.

Contents

Dedication iii

Foreword v

Chapter 1 : How to read you're map 1

Chapter 2 : The astrocartography or relocation map lines.
             What each of the lines (Asc or As, MC, Dsc or Dc and IC)
             represent 5

Chapter 3 : The As, AC, Asc or Ascendant lines....................................7

Chapter 4 : The Ds, DC, Dsc or Descendant lines 13

Chapter 5 : The MC, Mc or Midheaven lines 19

Chapter 6 : The IC, Ic or Nadir or lines 25

Chapter 7 : How can your astrocartogoraphy map be useful 31

Chapter 8 : Considering other astrological influences
             such as transits & progressions 33

1 : How to Read Your Map

FIRST, IF YOU DON'T ALREADY HAVE ONE, you'll need to purchase an astrocartogoraphy chart either on line or from a local astrologer. If you already have an astrology program such as Solar Fire that includes astrocartogoraphy you can go ahead and use that software to print out your relocation map. Alternatively, you can contact me Bud Barber or Bodhi Baba at 'Stargate Astrology services in the US: +1 (919) 985-1544 or Australia: +61 417 336 326 and for $20. (US) or $25. Australia. or: bud-barber@hotmail.com The information you'll need to already have and give the astrologer is your birth; time, date and place (city/town and country). If you do not have an accurate time of birth it would be best to wait until you can obtain that information before you order your astrocartogoraphy map. If you order one from me you will receive a map of the world as well as a blown-up map of the general area you live in, for example if you live in Boston, Mass. you'll receive a map of the world and a map of the US with your astrocartogoraphy lines superimposed over the top of them. If you live in London the blown-up map would be of Europe. If you live in Melbourne Australia the enlarged map will be of Australia and NZ. Once you have received your astrocartogoraphy chart then you're ready to go.

As you view your astrocartography chart or map, there are lines running all over a world. Each line is different. Some have a negative influence while others are positive. It would depend on the reason you're in that particular location, for example a Saturn/MC line may be quite good for your career but not so great for a vacation. All the Venus (MC, DC, ASC or IC) lines may be good for romance and social activity but not so good if you there for work or study. Therefore, the following text is to help you to interpret your own astrocartography chart. Though you're not knowledgeable in astrology, it's just a map with a lot of lines & symbols' running all over it that would have no meaning to you at this point.

Pictured on the left is a display of all the planets and their symbols as they're used in astrology. Note that two of the symbols Rahu (North Node) and Kethu (South Node) are not planets but still have an influence on areas of the world that you may either visit or live. Also, another 'planetoid' used in astrocartography is Chiron.' Its symbol pictured right and looks kind of like a key standing upright. However, its influence is somewhat weak, especially in comparison to the stronger planets and/or luminaries such as the Sun, Moon and the planet Saturn. Never the less it does have at least a noticeable effect on you at the locations it runs over on your relocation map. You'll also need to familiarize yourself with all the above symbols as your astrocartography map will only use the planetary symbols pictured here.

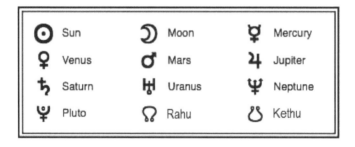

CHIRON

Though I will give a complete description of all the possible lines displayed on your map, the following is a general breakdown. If you'll notice on your map coupled with each planet symbol are the letters: MC, IC, AC and DC. They stand for; MC or Midheaven (10th house cusp), IC or Idiom Coeli (4th House cusp, AC or Ascendant (1st house cusp) and DC or Descendant (7th house cusp). These basically represent four fundamental areas of your life as follows:

- MC : Your career, work, goals, aspirations, achievements &/or education. It's sometimes associated to the Father Architype.

- IC : Your home base, family, domestic surroundings, unconscious and subjective world. It can also be associated to the Mother Architype.
- Asc : Your persona and your immediate environment. The way you come across or appear to others. The way you feel you need to be, in order to get by in the external world, society &/or your relationships.
- DC : Your marriage, partnerships, as well as other committed relationships. The reaction you generally attract from others and the external world in general.

So for example, if you have a Sun/IC line running through or near Miami Fla. USA, that particular line would affect you subjectively and/or your home/family life in Miami. If you're Sun were coupled with the DC line, that would affect your relationships there more than other areas of your life such as your career or family life.

The planets however would add different qualities to those locations, for example a Uranus/DC line running over a city that you only have a short stopover flight in, could cause unexpected disruptions such as flight cancelations, or lost luggage. I gave this example because it happened to me in a city that I had a Uranus line running directly over even though I was there only for a short time. Another interesting thing that's been known to happen is you may have a DC/Venus line – which is known to have very strong influence on love relationships – run over a place you've never visited before but you'll meet someone else who's from that city or town and even begin a relationship with them. So to conclude the lines (MC, IC, AC, & DC) that run all over the world map combined with a specific planet will not only give you descriptions of how you'll generally feel and experience that particular location but what exact area of life; home, career, relationships etc. that will affect you in.

One last thing that I should mention before I give all the various interpretations is, in order to have an accurate astrocartography chart reading you'll need to have an exact time of birth. So if you only have your mother's memory to go on you may not experience the graph as it reads. So check your birth certificate or hospital records if necessary because more than any other aspect of astrology, astrocartograph depends on an accurate birth time. Otherwise you may get a favourable reading for the Fiji Islands even though in reality that location actually lands somewhere in the middle of the South Pacific Ocean nowhere near Fiji itself.

Even though there are many different map designs and styles, your astrocartography chart or relocation map, should you already have one or order one in the future, will look something like this (pictured on right). Even though it may be slightly different basically the example I've given here should be the same. At an extra cost you can also order blow ups that zoom in on various areas of the globe such as; Asia, Australia/New Zealand, USA/Canada, Europe, Africa. The main map you'll receive will be a world map on one side with a zoom in on the area you're presently living on the other. The map I use will give the various planet symbols followed by; MC, IC, Asc or DC. You can next find the interpretations of all the possible combinations or lines in the subsequent texts.

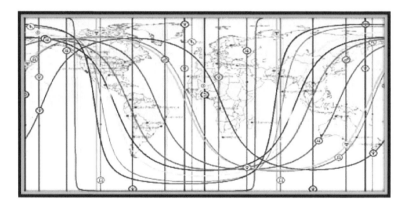

2 : The Astrocartography or Relocation Map Various Line Interpretations

Because of the restrictions of my computer instead of the planet symbol as it will appear on your astrocartogoraphy map, I have written the planet out as a word. Use the graph on page one to see the symbol if you do not already know them.

You'll notice there are four different lines (AS, DS, MC, IC) on the outer perimeter of your map. Each represents a different aspect or 'house' of your life, which can be interpreted as follows:

For the AS or Asc line the emphasis is on you and any planetary energy influencing this line. It largely determines your personality and therefore how you'd project yourself into the outside world at that particular location. For example, if you have an As/Venus line running through Boston Mass., then while living or visiting there you'd tend to have a more friendly amicable demeanour than you would at other locations not affected by this line. In other words, your persona has a tendency to take on the characteristics of whatever planet that's affecting you're As line location but only while visiting or living in that area. For example, in a place where you have an As/Jupiter line you'd be more playful and in the location you have an As/Saturn line you'd be more serious most of the time.

The Ds or Dsc line is more about you and others. Therefore, your partner and other relationships can play a very important role in these locations. For an example the Dsc/Venus line would be an excellent location to choose for a honeymoon, assuming of course that it lands in appropriate inhabitable places.

The MC or Mc line is about your conscious involvement with the outside objective world and your goals and ideas associated with that as opposed to your private, internal, subjective world. The planets that are

combined with this line give you an indication of the influence that location would have on your work/career as well as other external experiences,
activities and ambitions that you may have.

Where the Mc line land on your map has to do largely with your outer
or external life, the various IC lines are more associated to your internal
or subjective life. This consequently has a lot of influence on your home
and domestic life as well as your unconscious and aspects that your particular upbringing had on you. It will also affect your family relationships
as well as colour the perception of your mother archetype. Therefore, depending on the planet combined with this line it could affect your present
living situation, your moods, feelings, emotions in many different ways as
well as your relationship with parents and family in general.

Basically, the lines that you'll see stretched all over your relocation map
represent the main angles in your chart, which are as they appear on my
maps; your Ascendant (As), Descendant (Ds), Midheaven (Mc) and your
Nadir or Idem Coli (Ic). The As & Ds represent the eastern and western
horizon and the MC & IC, the exact point directly above (the heavens)
and below (the Earth) at the ecliptic (the plane that the planets rotate on
around the Sun). For example, if you were born at 12 noon, you'd have the
Sun conjunct your MC when you were born, if you were born at sunset,
you'd have Sun opposition your Ascendant or Sun conjunct Ds.

At the extreme ends or North & South Poles of your relocation chart
you'll notice all the lines on the map seem to converge in one small location. This occurs on all astrocartography charts and even though in areas
where there are more lines coming together you would get a stronger influence, the areas on the globe this occurs on are so remote and extremely
north or south that the influence in most cases should be considered ir-
relevant to you personally.

One last note; a line by itself does not represent the entire zone of influence. The effect extends to either side for quite some distance. So, if a
line runs directly over a town there can still be some influence as much as
approximately 100 miles or 160 kilometres to either side of that towns'
location. So, to give you some idea of that distance, if a line were to run
north to south directly through the centre of Florida the influence of that
line would easily have an effect on you if you were located on either the
Atlantic Ocean or the Gulf of Mexico side of Fla. This would be especially
true of the Sun and Moon lines, as the luminaries are always somewhat
stronger than the planets.

3 : The Ac, Asc or Ascendant + Planet Lines

AC OR ASC/SUN : Of all the possible Astrocartography locations this one can be the most self-centred causing you to be more focussed on yourself and your own concerns and affairs than on any other location line. This can of course be either good or bad depending on your circumstances. if you're with a partner and or others who require even a reasonable amount of your time and attention there could be problems as you could to be accused of being selfish and only concerned with your own needs and desires and if you live on this line it even becomes more of a problem as it could build up even more over time. However, if you're only passing through and normally a very giving and considerate individual traveling to a location on this line may be a good opportunity for you to have some 'me time' to regenerate and look after yourself for a change. Whether living there or just passing through you're likely to feel more self-confident, extroverted enthusiastic and generally feel more energised than usual.

AC/MOON : Even though you're moody and have a tendency to be more emotional, this location could easily be quite relaxing and comfortable for you as you're more able to maintain warm feelings of security and emotional wellbeing. As opposed to the Sun, here you're more likely to be introverted than out going but your ability to feel empathy and care for others are also greatly heightened. It's a good area to consider for your home base if you're looking to move to some place long term as well. It's also possible while traveling to a place that's influenced by the Moon line to feel more nostalgic and even miss and long for your old home environment and family. Within yourself here you're feel more comfortable and concerned more about the wellbeing of others,

AC/MERCURY : While the Moon line is more emotional, here you tend to be more dry, mental and intellectual. Even if you live at this location you feel more alert and interested in your surroundings and interact more with others than at most other places. For example, this would be an ideal location to study, attend a university or even compete in a chess tournament. My advice is if you travel to an Asc/Mercury location to bring a lot of books and reading material. You're also likely to find you're more mentally active and talkative than usual as well. I notice that when I'm on a Ac/Mercury line I spend a lot more time on the computer and corresponding and talking with others.

AC/VENUS : In the Asc/Venus locations you are more loving, friendly, generally have a positive mood as well as feeling romantic. Therefore, you're much more emotional than you would be under the influence of the previous Mercury line. This is a great place to go on vacation but not so well if you need to work hard because with Venus influencing you there's more of a tendency to be playful and indulgent, therefore be careful not become overly sexually indulgent, eat, drink &/or spend too much money. You are more prone to initiate new friendships and/or relationships here as well.

AC/MARS : If I were an athlete such as a tennis player who travels all over the world, this would be a location I'd really want to compete as opposed to relaxing on a beach. Under the effects of this line you're more energetic, competitive and goal oriented. However here you can also be more aggressive, angry, impatient, impulsive and accident prone. So even if you're only visiting such a place, keep active but you may also need to do something such as yoga to relieve all your tension. Your sex drive here is also likely to be more noticeable.

AC/JUPITER : At these locations whether living here or just visiting, you're much more likely to be light, optimistic, enthusiastic and maintain an expanded view of the world. Your mood though playful at times can also be idealistic and creative. You seem to be more accepting of everything and have the capacity to enjoy life no matter what twists and turns in the road you may take. Your experience at almost any location, no matter what the reason whether it's your home or visiting, is improved by this influence.

AC/SATURN : Some might think that a place influenced by the Asc/Saturn line is negative no matter what but that's not entirely true. If this line runs over a location where you're pursuing a high-level career, then it can be very beneficial as your more disciplined and focussed here than in other locations. True you're more likely to become more Saturnine in nature which is serious, solemn and even withdrawn therefore this place is probably not the ideal location for your dream holiday. Also, if you're a person who's prone to depression, then this area on the map should be avoided at all costs. Only if you are a positive, optimistic individual by nature would you be able to exist here for any length of time. Also, at this location you may also find that circumstances limit, restrict and block your endeavours more than in most other places so you may have to work harder here in order to get things done.

AC/CHIRON : Because under AC/Chiron you're drawn to self-healing, reflection and spiritual matters any place in which you'd like to pursue that sort of lifestyle is best wherever this line happens to land or cross over on your map. Under this influence you're more prone to be sincere, interested in deep & meaningful conversations and meditation. If you travelled somewhere to attend a health retreat, undertake psychotherapy or simply to withdraw from the tensions of everyday living this would be the exact location you'd want to choose. Here you may also find your past memories seem to flood out of nowhere into your conscious mind.

AC/URANUS : At this place wherever it happens to land on your relocation map if you're normally a calm &/or focussed person you can expect to feel very different from your usual self, assuming you do not live here. If you're already generally hyper, mentally scattered &/or disorganized, this locality could turn you into a chaotic bundle of nerves and in a constant state of change and confusion. For as long as he stayed there, one client of mine described it like having a temporary case of attention deficit disorder, place or as I call it, 'scatter-brained.' This could be a positive location however if you make an effort to remain focussed then you could entertain a variety of activities, multi task without becoming distracted, and feel mentally stimulated. This place could be a location where you experience a lot of excitement and adventure and things change for the positive.

AC/NEPTUNE : There's a number of ways this location could make you feel. Dazed, confused and disorientated is one possibility, while another is strolling around nonstop during your time there with a case of chronic jet lag. You could also feel hyper sensitive here which could cause you to seek refuge or be overly defensive or protective. Some other more positive effects could be you'd feel deep peaceful introspective and more meditative. If it were possible this would be an excellent location to travel to for a meditation retreat; you could just sit and do nothing and just let the planet Neptune transport you to higher levels of consciousness. It's also a good location for vacations where you only want to do little more than lay on the beach and relax. The AC/Neptune line or locality is also a good place to access your creativity imagination and intuition. You could find yourself day dreaming here more than usual and your dreams themselves more vivid and meaningful.

AC/PLUTO : In general a Pluto line could be one of those places you live or visit that can change you &/or your life permanently. I remember one person telling me, "I'll never be the same after visiting there." The AC/Pluto location specifically causes Pluto to be stronger in your personality than usual. There are several symptoms of Pluto having more of an influence over you than usual. You generally feel more intense about everything: you may become obsessed with some things that ordinarily would not be of an interest to you and you may feel a stronger libido coming from a deep primal level of your being. Yet you may gain piercing insight into people and situations that could astonish and amaze others. You could also become very concerned about life death and the deeper meaning of existence in general. While traveling if you're not already having a Pluto influence from some other source such a transit and you start to feel this way, then you've probably landed on a Pluto line. It's a good place to intentionally go for self –transformation as you will feel more inclined to become an agent of permanent change. Working with others here also makes you feel more empowered.

AC/RAHU : Even though these lines (Rahu and Kathu) are not as significant as most of the others they're still important. Asc/Rahu or North Node can give you a forward-looking perspective and therefore be a location where you seek to improve yourself by letting go of the past and moving forward.

AC/KATHU : This line is thought by many astrologers to be locations where you are prone to act out past life tendencies. This can be detrimental in helping you to evolve depending on your motives. Though if you become caught in a repetitive loop it can be harmful to any further growth. However, if you become aware of these old habits and seek to transcend them it's of course positive.

4 : The Ds, Dsc or Descendant + Planet Lines

DS/SUN : Depending on how social you already are, you could be far more outgoing and interactive with people friends' partners than you normally are. You generally assume and therefore mostly experience that people are more drawn to you and see you in a positive light here as opposed to other locations. Your relationships as well as other acquaintances seem to carry more of a positive charge here and even if you're normally a shy withdrawn individual, here you tend to come out of hiding more and shine with greater self-confidence. Therefore, the effect this location could have on you, via your increased interaction with others, reveals more of yourself to them; you get to know everyone here whether permanent or just passing through much more than you ordinarily would in most other locations. Here you value your partnerships, relationships, friendships more than usual and are willing to go out of your way to maintain them. Here it's important to keep your needs in balance with the needs of others because if they do become disproportionate the upset you experience will also be greater as well; the universe tends to be a true reflection of your own self more than in other places so you can learn a lot about yourself by what you attract in others.

DS/MOON : Like the Ds/Sun line your attention tends to be less on yourself and more on others but instead, in a caring, nurturing and empathetic way. You are also easily influenced by the emotional state of others, so someone in a good mood could easily bring you out of a melancholy or withdrawn state of being. You're more prone to express and share your feelings with others and therefore you tend to attract people who are emotionally demonstrative and concerned and kind in nature. It's also possible however that you attract some acquaintances that are moody and irritable, if so, you should consider this to be a reflection of your own conscious or unconscious inner feelings. Relationships under this line will also take on more of a nurturing and emotional nature.

DS/MERCURY : The conversations and communications you have with others here are likely to be cerebral and mentally stimulating. Regardless of whether these interactions are social or just purely technical, you're likely to gain a lot of insight from those you exchange ideas with. This is also prone to be a location for whatever reason that stimulates you mentally, therefore it is like all the other Mercury lines a good location for study, writing, teaching and public speaking. Others may experience you as dry and intellectual than in other locations. Communication is stimulated and enhanced to any relationship under the effect of this line.

DS/VENUS : If you're looking for love this is the best place for that. Even if you are a bit prickly in nature your company in this location is pleasant and enjoyable for others who happen to be around you here. You'll most likely have a warm, loving effect on others in this area and people tend to be more agreeable and affectionate while interacting with you. This is also a place where you're most likely to either find or visit with a romantic partner while probably having a positive outcome. For example, if you're traveling here you might meet the partner you eventually marry or begin a lifelong relationship with. This is so because at this location you tend to be more attracted to the people you meet and they to you as well. It can also be a place that brings out your indulgent nature and therefore you tend to focus more on play rather than other interests such as hard work. If you were to travel for a honeymoon it's good to know that your relationships can become more sexual and deeply romantic.

DS/MARS : I would not say avoid the locations near this line but while you're here you'd certainly need to be careful of becoming too aggressive and argumentative. You can be more prone to accidents here and others may find you abrupt irritating and too wilful, therefore either avoid you or respond in a very unpleasant manner. There is a positive side to this location and that is it energises you. If you are normally a passive, easy-going or lethargic person then this location could give you the courage to become forceful in life. If you're already an aggressive or wilful person, you'll need to watch out here as you could end up, in some serious conflict or confrontations. If you are in a relationship under the Ds/Mars line it is much more prone to anger and conflict. One last warning even if you feel you're in a stable pleasant mood, you may feel as if everyone around you is hostile and argumentative. Try not to get sucked in to their negativity, or if traveling you can simply move onto another location.

Ds/Jupiter : Those you encounter here find you open, expansive and in-spirational. Not only that but this location brings out those qualities in you and therefore you have a positive effect on others. Your relationships with friends, associates and acquaintances at this location are quite posi-tive, fun and can bring opportunities for both you and those you en-counter. For example, you could meet someone who offers you a business opportunity here or gives you support and encouragement. If you were to play the part of a teacher, Guru or mentor to others this would be an ideal location as the overall effect you have on others is inspiring. Relationships under this line are generally enhanced and improved.

DS/SATURN : This is not the greatest location for social interactions in the way that Venus, Sun and Jupiter would be. In fact, here, especially if you already have a sombre disposition, to other people you could seem to be far too serious, withdrawn or even depressed. Therefore people, or at least those seeking lighter interactions with others, would probably avoid interacting or being around you. On the other hand, if you're by na-ture playful and don't take life seriously enough, such a location could help you to mature, grow up a bit and become responsible. So, the inter-actions you encounter here could be harsh, difficult and challenging. Compared to other places you are much less drawn to a social life and could become quite withdrawn. This is a good location to initiate serious commitments or go to events such as meditation retreats; however, it could also even be a place where you may find yourself being incarcerated or held in detention.

DS/CHIRON : Healing relationships such as doctor/patient or thera-pist/client are important for all of us and it is here on this line that you may encounter the development such an interaction, including that of a partner. Here you may find that you're more able to fit into either role, the healer or the one being healed, than at other locations. You may be a teacher or become a student. Your encounters with others are also more likely to take on a spiritual quality wherever this line influences you on the globe. Any relationship under Chiron's effect is likely to experience deep healing.

DS/URANUS : Relationships with others can be extreme, exciting but also short lived at this location. This could either be good or frustrating depending on your wants and needs at the time. If you want stability it can be frustrating but if it's freedom and independence you want then this could be just the kind of place you've been looking for. If traveling to a Ds/Uranus location with a partner the two of you could grow distant and apart during this time seeking freedom to grow and change on your own. You are also more rebellious under the Ds/Uranus line so be careful not to stir up too much trouble and be flexible as there will be many unexpected changes here.

DS/NEPTUNE : Anyone seeking deep spiritual encounters between themselves and others or spiritual relationships such as the Guru Disciple relationship should consider going to the locations on your map in which this line runs. For example, I have a Neptune line running through the area of India that I met my Guru and lived for many years. However, any relationship or relationships that you happen to have under the influence of the Dc/Neptune line is likely to take on a more spiritual quality. Your interactions with others here are likely to become more refined and sensitive to those in other locations, therefore some of your deepest encounters whether spiritual or mundane could develop under the influence of Ds/Neptune line. However, on the negative side the influence at this location can be confusing disorientating and lower your overall energy level. For whatever reason your communications may become distorted and/or vague and therefore it's not the greatest place for precise direct interaction. Though, if you just want to go somewhere with your loved one, lie on the beach and do nothing its perfect.

DS/PLUTO : This location has good and bad effects on any partner you happen to be with as well as your encounters with others. On the negative side it can pit you against others causing suspicion, manipulation, obsessiveness and power struggles. On the positive side it can intensify your sexual relationship(s) and through your interactions with others you'll notice you tend to have a great deal of personal and spiritual transformation. Some people you encounter here could treat you with mistrust, while others see you as a deeply spiritual individual that's had a permanent impact on their lives. This could cause the people you meet here to be lastingly changed by interacting with you and vice versa. While traveling through such locations you should avoid dangerous situations and conflict with local authorities. The main difficulty is people here tend to project their unresolved shadow issues onto you and you as well could do the same with them. This can lead to personal power struggles between you and others.

DS/RAHU : Through the interaction you have with people here you resolve past karmas and therefore move toward your life purpose. You could find this allows you to more easily let go of the past (especially relationships of the past) and move forward.

DS/KATHU : You may feel that this location or the people you meet here, even though you may have never been here before, seem vaguely familiar. This could be because it's a place that you lived during a past life and/or some of the people you meet here are people you've met in previous incarnations. It's also very possible that you could meet someone from a city/town or country indicated by this line that you feel you have a strong past life connection to. For example, you feel you have a strong past life connection to Russia and you marry someone from St. Petersburg

5 : The Mc, MC or Midheaven + Planet Lines

MC/SUN : As a place to pursue a career as well as other ambitions this is an excellent location. You are likely to go about achieving your goals with a great deal of self-confidence under the influence of the MC/Sun line. Here you are more likely than in other locations to put a great deal of energy into accomplishing your goals. This is partially due to the fact that here you have more optimism, ambition and energy than in other locations to begin with. Especially careers that involve a public life, such as acting and the media, you'd surely expect to succeed in. At the very least there would certainly be less fear of failure and a sense that the environment or world around is supportive of your success. Even if you're not here for career reasons, your energy is high, mood is positive and you shine forth with enthusiasm.

MC/MOON : Any career especially in the fields of healing, naturopathy, medicine, nursing, catering or the food industry, real estate or any scenario that involves looking after and healing others this line would certainly enhance and support. Even areas of endeavour in your life that do not fall under those specific areas it would still allow you to adjust and feel comfortable with whatever you were doing. In general, it allows you to accomplish your goals with ease and comfort. It can however bring your emotions more into play than say other lines and if your mood were to be negative that could be harmful and vice versa. In all external activities in general under the MC/Moon line there's a noticeable tendency to nurture, heal, assist and look after others.

MC/MERCURY : For intellectuals and others who depend mostly on their mind to flourish in their careers, living under this line would only increase their abilities to succeed. However even for those who do not pursue intellectual careers this aspect can still be helpful as the mind's abilities are greatly improved. The only possible way I can imagine it wouldn't be so helpful is for someone who depends mostly on their psychic or intuitive abilities and in that case an overly active mind could interfere with a situation that requires a quiet mind. It should also go without saying that this would be a helpful aspect to anyone attending school or a university as a student, therefore when applying to a school or university for higher education this line should be taken into serious consideration. Career aside this aspect can cause someone living under its influence to identify strongly with their mind.

MC/VENUS : For people perusing a creative education or careers in the Arts this line is more important than the previous MC/Mercury line as it empowers that area of their life. For example, I know of a famous actor/comedian who attended the Juilliard School of the Performing Arts and his MC/Venus line runs right over New York City which is the location of that school and certainly his attainment there contributed to his eventual success. The only negative thing I could say about this line is it can be a bit lethargic and unambitious, even though perhaps not as much as MC/Neptune. Venus being the ruler of Taurus and Libra it can also enhance one's career in social work, one on one counselling or even sex workers (Libra) while the Taurus side of this Venus influence could improve work in; sales, designers, interior decorators and even financial advisors. Whether male or female this aspect can cause you to identify more with the feminine side of your Psyche at least in this region.

MC/MARS : Where MC/Venus can enhance identification with the feminine, the MC/Mars influence tips the scales so to speak, more in the masculine direction, at least in this location. Even though Dsc/Mars and Asc/Mars can be negative, this is the one line (MC/Mars) that is almost entirely positive as Mars energies combine favourably with career and ambition. However, if someone were to travel somewhere for other reasons such as for a vacation then this line could still cause conflict and trouble as it can cause one's ego energies to run high. On the other hand, if this aspect energizes the place where you're pursuing your career, it can give strength, focus, wilfulness to succeed and the persistence to obtain that success. This is especially true if the individual with MC/Mars were a professional athlete, coach, trainer, or was to pursue a technical career such as an engineer or a mathematician. In general, it can make you more ambitious and competitive than usual so depending on the job that could be a plus or a minus.

MC/JUPITER : Of all the lines that could help and enhance ones career no matter what their line of work, MC/Jupiter is the one that seems to bring the most success. It brings out a positive attitude toward one's profession and when perusing one's career there's also generally a noticeable optimism with an assured feeling that the sky is the limit. Living under this aspect is unlikely to have its enthusiasm curbed no matter what the setback. The only negative side is it sees success in a broad sense and if the person living under a MC/Mars line isn't careful there can be a tendency to overlook important details that can cause problems & obstructions in the long run. It can also cause such an individual fail to see something that is a problem, as a problem, if he/she is not careful. Someone living in a place with a MC/Jupiter line running through it is more prone to take life seriously and identify with the clown or trickster archityep.

MC/SATURN : Normally Saturn lines are considered to be malefic or negative however in the case of Saturn combined with your Midheaven the reverse is true. In this location you're more likely to have the self-discipline to focus and establish yourself effectively in your chosen career. It can also assist you in being decisive and more organized so that success is much more likely. Where the previous line, MC/Jupiter, can help bring you opportunities that lead to success, the MC/Saturn line gives you the tenacity and capacity for endurance and hard work that often lead to high levels of achievement. The only thing that you'd need to watch out for under the influence of this line is becoming so engrossed in your work that you have very little free time for anything else in other words becoming a 'workaholic.' So, if you are free to pick the location to peruse a serious career then without a doubt the areas covered by the MC/Saturn line would be ideal. Living here you tend to take life more seriously.

MC/CHIRON : If you live in a location influenced by this line, just as with the MC/Moon, then you're more likely to be successful especially if you're in the health and healing profession. This applies not only to your work in this profession but your studies as well. However not only this location is helpful with a career in the areas of health, medicine and healing, it's also very strong for students & teachers of spiritual subjects such as a hatha yoga and meditation. Also, even if your studies are not biology or teacher related and you're into something entirely different such as engineering just like the MC/Mercury line the MC/Chiron location is a very powerful place to undertake any study no matter what the subject is. Even if you are just passing through such an area, you're more likely to identify with the mentor and be prone to helping other people out. At this location no matter what your line of work, you tend to identify more with the teacher/healer side of your personality.

MC/URANUS : For people who're engineers, scientists, astrologers, or into computer and internet technology or even an electrical engineer, then this is an ideal location, as it enhances the higher brain functions that enable 'left-brain' orientated men & women to excel in this sort of career. It can also be a useful line to live under for the study and practice of high-level scientific professions such as astrophysics,' quantum physics,' and/or theoretical mathematicians. Life in this location whether it's on your MC/Asc line, your permanent residence or just temporary, is more likely to become chaotic, unpredictable and occasionally confusing. Therefore, if you move to such a region it might take some getting used to, otherwise unless you can manage to become more focussed, you'll develop a short attention span, become scattered and, 'a bit all over the place.' Because MC not only has to do with career but ego as well under this influence it causes you to identify more with the radical free spirit who prefers constant change and freedom such as the anarchist, rather than security and stability.

MC/NEPTUNE : This is certainly not the type of location you'd choose to live if you're undertaking an ordinary career such as; an electrician, professional athlete or accountant as you'd find yourself spacing out allot and that could get you into a great deal of trouble if you were, for example a brain surgeon. However, if you're a psychic, spiritual teacher, tarot card reader or perhaps a highly creative writer, poet, artist, musician or anyone working in a field that requires a powerful creative imagination, the influence this location would have on you would definitely be an asset to your work. Paul Simon who has a powerful Neptune aspect to Midheaven in his birth chart once said, "I'm glad I never listened to my teachers who told me not to day dream in class, because it's precisely that state that I go into in which I've written some of my best songs." Besides career anyone who's perusing a spiritual life and prefers to dissolve their ego rather than build it up this would be an excellent location for them to live. Under this line you are more prone to identify with your higher consciousness rather than the ego. Its also s good location to visit to have a relaxing vacation.

MC/PLUTO : Living on or near a MC/Pluto line you see yourself more as a force of death, rebirth and transformation. Identification with such a powerful force can cause many permanent changes in your life as well as the people and friends you associate with in that area. Pluto can be connected to many different kinds of work & careers, from a psychiatrist to a private decretive or a mortician who works in funeral parlours to a cancer researcher who works in scientific laboratories. These may all seem to be very different but they all have one thing in common, life, death and transformation; looking deeper than the surface to discover the truth. If your career has any of these archetypical themes running through it, then it's quite likely the MC/Pluto line would strengthen and enhance your career while living under its influence. Living on or near this line could also have the effect of breaking down your ego and depending on whether you see this as a good or bad thing this could have a positive or negative influence on your life.

MC/RAHU : Living on or near this line may help you achieve your life goals and ambitions easier especially those which are career related. It can also help you resolve past memories and impressions, as far back as early childhood or even past lives. The MC/Rahu line is also said to be a good indication of locations you may have lived in during your previous incarnations.

MC/KATHU : The effect of this line can help you to draw from hidden talents and abilities that you've forgotten about or you're for whatever reason are no longer in touch with. For example, a friend of mine when he moved to a location under the influence of MC/Kathu started to remember a past life as an artist which then started to contribute to his work as an artist in this life. Experiences such as these can begin to broaden the scope of your understanding of who you are.

6 - The Ic, IC or Nadir + Planet Lines

IC OR IC/SUN : Since your internal state of being is more pronounced on this line, as opposed to the MC line where your external life is more the focus, this is an ideal place to experience a positive, lighter, more complete sense of wellbeing. Self-confidence seems to come easy for you here so while under the effects of this line success in whatever you do just comes naturally. You'll also notice that here you have more energy and greater vitally so you'll most likely not have to worry about health issues as might be the case if you lived or visited somewhere else. Here your domestic life and relationships with family members is also positive and conflicts that you may have encountered in other locations here seem to just disappear. If just visiting here, for the entire time you'll probably notice how enthusiastic and uplifted you feel during your stay.

IC/MOON : This is considered to be one of the best line locations to live under in terms of domestic tranquillity, security and happiness. Because you feel so much at home and comfortable at this location even if you only visit here for a short while it can still feel warm and welcoming and therefore a lot like home to you. So, if you're primary concern in life is to settle down, raise a family in an area of the world where your surroundings are harmonious, pleasant and mostly enjoyable then a location or locations indicated by this line are excellent places for you to consider, as long as moving to and living at these places is possible. Also, if you've recently retired and looking for a comfortable, secure place to live the rest of your life, then this line and where it runs through on your map will probably give you some of the best locations to achieve that goal. Also, on the IC/Moon line you're usually more in touch with your moods, feelings and emotions, therefore your life and the decisions you make here will be influenced by these more than in other locations.

IC/MERCURY : Confidence in your rational thinking mind is stronger here, therefore an excellent place for study, reading, doing research as well as communication and teaching others. If you happen to be doing studies or other intellectual activities at this location, you should take to your studies more naturally and find it much easier than at most other places. If you live here your home environment is quite likely to become filled with things such as computers, books, chess boards etc. that keep you mentally stimulated, active and aware. Also, your family relationships, at least for you, will require greater communication as well as mental interactions, debates and discussions on various subjects than other locations. Sometimes however you may start to feel a bit dry and impersonal and if this happens you may need to get away so that you can regain a connection to your more emotional, intuitive or spiritual self. Translating your inner feelings into words and then communicating them to others should come easier to you here than at other places.

IC/VENUS : Sometimes we need another person to connect to the feeling of love, here however the state of love can just well up from within you for no particular reason at all. Whether you live here or are just visiting, it will take a lot more than usual to upset you and your overall mood in most cases will be warm, friendly and loving for the minority of time. You seem to attract abundance to yourself here as well so feelings of scarcity and that something is missing is unlikely. You're probably able to see value in things you ordinarily wouldn't and thus find ways of attracting more opportunities to yourself than usual. If you travel to this location with a loved one not only will you feel more in line with your partner, you'll feel this way about the land the people and all your surroundings as well.

IC/MARS : There are not many places I'd say to avoid as all things in the spectrum of experience are of value, however this is probably one of them. At this location or locations effected by the IC/Mars line you could find yourself becoming so critical (mostly self-critical), irritable, frustrated and angry at things that ordinarily do not upset you that you cannot enjoy any time that you spend here. Things just simply have a tendency to go wrong here and it seems you have to spend an enormous amount of time and energy just to keep things from degenerating into a chaotic mess. However, there are some exceptions. This location could be good for you if you are a rather lethargic, apathetic sort of a person. If so, this location could motivate you a bit or build a fire under you to use the energy of this planet to wake you up. For example, if you're the sort of person who never seems to have the self-confidence to stand up for yourself, then this location could give you enough courage to quit being so mild and fearful and instead deal with the people bullying you. If you live on this line and your home life has always been full of anger and conflict then you may consider moving somewhere else.

IC/JUPITER : Unlike the IC/Mars line you'd want to place yourself on locations that this line crosses over as much as possible and if you live on the IC/Jupiter line even better. Some people find their 'dream home' on or near this line and the relations with their family members here are also quite positive and beneficial as well. Others realize it's the perfect location for a vacation and when you are here for no particular reason, you'd most likely feel positive self-confident and quite optimistic for most of the time. While traveling through a IC/Jupiter location you commonly feel lucky and everything seems to works out in your favour, even if normally you don't feel that you're a lucky person in particular. I've also noticed that many people find what it is they've been looking for on locations near or on this line, which is why it's sometimes called 'the line of opportunity.' So, whether living here or just passing through in most cases this place will likely be expansive, positive and uplifting for you. The only thing you need to watch out for however is excess. It is possible to spend too much money, eat or drink too much and then regret it later.

IC/SATURN : Whether you're traveling or live here, another line that in most cases should be avoided is the IC/Saturn line. The first thing that comes to mind when I think of the influence of this line is depression. I feel you'd have to be a super positive individual to endure living permanently on this line. The Saturn influence on your home and family life in particular could be unbearable. I know someone who lived on a IC/Saturn line for 29 years, then he'd finally had enough and moved to a better location. His description of that was, "Like going from a dungeon into an enchanted forest." If you're just traveling through an area influenced by this line, while you're there, you'll probably wonder why am I worrying so much, or why do I feel so trapped, confined and unenthusiastic or what's happened to my '*joie de vivre*.' If under a Saturn line that does happen, before you get stuck, stop worrying about it, and just get as far away from there as you can, otherwise Saturn can be like quicksand and has a way of making you feel like you should do this or that or you become obligated to stay for whatever reasons. On the other hand, if I had to think of something positive about the IC/Saturn line I'd say; it could help give you the self-discipline necessary to lose a lot of weight or if it were the case, to get your life organized from a state of chaos or it could help you accomplish some monumental task that ordinarily you'd not be capable of achieving.

IC/CHIRON : This is a good location to live or travel to for self-healing. Whether you live here or are just visiting your focus is more on self-improvement and healing. This includes spiritual, mental and physical health. I knew of someone who had severe allergies so they found a place that they would be less affected by pollen dust and all the external things they were allergic to and moved there. As a result, his health improved dramatically and when we did his astrocartography chart the new location landed right on his IC/Chiron line. However not only can living under the influence of this line improve your health and state of mind it can also bring out the healer as well as the teacher in you. At this location your internal state of being is likely to be more like that of a teacher &/or healer, and cause you to help others close to you especially those in your family.

IC/URANUS : This line could help someone develop spiritual understanding since Uranus is associated to the higher spiritual mind, however it could also create much restlessness and internal agitation. The problem at this location is the IC line would affect you on the subjective level and that in turn could disrupt your home and family situation. So, without a peaceful inner life and a chaotic home life it wouldn't usually give way to inner peace and deep meditation. If you're just visiting an IC/Uranus location it's likely you will not stay there for very long as you may become so restless that you could bolt at the first opportunity. However, if the Uranus line causes life to change unexpectedly in a way that makes that place seem interesting and more exciting then you could possibly stay on longer. In order to remain in an IC/Uranus location for a stretch of time you'd probably have to overcome your need for constant change and restlessness and focus on the more important aspects of your life.

IC/NEPTUNE : You could say that all the trans-Saturnine planet lines (the IC line in particular) from Chiron to Pluto are very likely to have more or less of a spiritual effect on you, that is as long as you're sensitive enough to be influenced by them, as the outer planets can sometimes be too subtle to notice. Of all of the trans-Saturnine planet lines however the IC/Neptune is the strongest spiritually and even though its influence could be useful for other things such as imaginative, creative undertakings, it's by far more useful and effective with spiritual endeavours. So, if I were to find the ideal ashram to retreat to and complete my *sadhana* (spiritual practices), I'd certainly hope to have a IC/Saturn line running directly over or nearby that location. If someone were to live under this line, they would not be motivated to do much or become addicted to alcohol and/or drug use rather than spiritual activities. There'd need to be a balance of self-discipline and spirituality in order for this influence to work well. If wanted to retire and move from your present location the places this line crosses over would probably be the primary locations you would be happiest to spend your senior years.

IC/PLUTO : Since all IC lines affect you more internally than externally like the IC/Saturn line your overall mood is likely to be heavier serious and intense. This is not to say that this location is not useful for anything, for example it's extremely expedient for deep therapeutic soul searching, looking at one's life under a cold light, most any form of self–transformation and meditation. Though, your time here is most likely not going to be spent going to parties and having a good time. For whatever reason if needed to have time alone and reflect on the important issues of your life visiting this particular location would be a very wise choice. For some people, living here full time could become a bit dreary and depressing unless you could find some 'larger than life' project to dedicate your life to. You'd also have a tendency to focus on the negatives of life, such as death, suffering and loneliness, and as a result this would probably become a setting for you to manifest that all around you for as long as you reside here.

IC/RAHU : Whether you live here or are just visiting, you can easily recall and reflect on your past; some of these memories may even be from a previous life or incarnations. Hence you have a better intuitive sense of the direction you presently need to focus on in order to attain a greater balance and your life goals.

IC/KATHU : Your sense of accomplishment may feel more complete here and you may even recall some of these successes from this and previous lives. Here however your goals are more internal than external so living under the influence of this line will help you to find this state of subjective peace. If you do not live here this could be a good location to at least travel to for example, to write your memoirs. Of all the lines in Astrocartogoraphy this one is probably the strongest indicator of where you may have lived in some of your recent past lives. For example, if you have the IC/Kathu or south node line running through say Berlin and you feel a strong connection to Germany then it's quite likely you may have lived there in your past life or at least some recent previous incarnation.

7 : How Can Your Astrocartography Map Be More Useful?

FIRST YOU SHOULD ANALYSE the place you are presently living. Find the location on your map and see what lines if any run over or near the city, town or location where you live. Read the text or texts if there's more than one line near you and that should give you a fairly good description of the affects living there have on you. It will probably tell you things you already know, but as you can become accustomed to an influence over time you may not be as aware of it after a while. It's when you leave such a location that it becomes obvious what its affects had been on you.

Next you have to ask yourself, what do I want from where I live? What's most important to me? If it's career and activities in the outside world then you'd want to read the Mc lines. If it's your subjective or internal state of being and your home/family life then you need to read the text for the various planets in your Ic line. If it's relationships and other partnerships such as a business partner then have a look at the Dc or Descendant lines. And finally, if it's you, you personally and the way you project yourself into the world or how you come across to others that's more important, then look at the interpretations of the various Asc lines.

Then this should help you choose a particular line and give you an indication of where the optimum location is for you to live. However, you may not want to relocate but are just looking for a place to visit for a while. In that case look at the various places you think you'd like to visit and then read the descriptions of the lines if any, running over or near it. If there's no lines crossing over, within 500 miles of the location either side, then that's not a negative thing, it just means that place has no effect on you either way. Its influence is just neutral.

One thing you should keep in mind is, it depends on why you're traveling to a specific location in relation to what line you pick. If you need to go to a university to earn a degree then you wouldn't want to travel to a Venus line location. You'd want something that would help out academically such as Ds or Mc/Mercury line. Also, if you've already decided where you want to study then you'd want to check that location to see if it supports your education. If not then you might consider looking for a different University at a different location. Read the line or lines that go over the place where you want to live, work, have a romance, travel to for vacation etc. and use your map to pick the optimum places.

Last but not least, countries that have many lines running through them are probably places in the world that you're drawn to for whatever reason. Places that do not have many lines could be areas that would not be of much interest to you even if you live there. The place that you were born incidentally is the location where you can experience the true nature of your birth chart as you can in no other location. For example, if you were born in Brooklyn NY but move away for whatever reason when you return there, you'd probably always get a sense of being the true you, whatever that means to you.

8 : Considering Other Astrological Influences Such as Transits & Progressions

IT GOES WITHOUT SAYING a negative location such as Mars/Dc or Saturn/IC would be the last place you'd want to visit during a difficult transit like Pluto opposition Moon. That would only compound the difficulties making your experience unbearable at least during the time of the negative transits or progressions. Therefore, it's not only a good idea to study and know your astrocartography chart but to keep in touch with your various influences throughout time as well. Otherwise you may visit a place because you've studied your relocation map and found it to be one of the best places in the world for you to live and then wonder when you get there why you feel so bad. It could be because you forgot to check your transits that showed troublesome transits and/or progressions going on at the same time.

Where astrocartography influences you in terms of space or your location in the world, transits, progressions and return charts influence you throughout time. It is not within the range of this book to delineate all the various transits, progressions and returns however you should always keep in mind that even in the best of locations such as; Jupiter/Asc, Sun/MC or Venus/Dc, a detrimental transit or transits such as your Saturn return &/or your progressed Moon opposition Mars could turn what would normally have been a pleasant experience or exciting adventure into a negative, disappointing experience. Therefore, don't think that just because you move to say Phoenix Arizona because your astrocartography map gives that location as one of the best places in the world for you to live that all your problems will be forever resolved. While you're living there you still have to go through all the various time related influences just like everyone else. However, the better location would still make the load seem a lot lighter than it would if you were to experience them somewhere else.

However, the reverse is also true. Positive transits such as Jupiter conjunct Venus or progressed Sun trine Jupiter would be heightened and better experienced than they would at most other places. For example, I know of a lady who travelled to a Venus on her Descendant location (Venus/Dc) and during that time she had Jupiter conjunct her Venus in the 7th house of marriage and partnership. While she was there, she met and fell in love with the man she ultimately married. Up until this day she says that this was one of the most enjoyable periods of her life. She and her husband return to that place almost every year for their anniversary.

Bud Barber or Bodhi Baba is a professional Astrologer as well as a world traveller who's been practicing and conducting research in the field of astrology for over 40 years. He currently lives in Melbourne Australia & Raleigh NC, USA where he teaches courses in astrology, runs workshops & gives private consultations. Having once been the personal astrologer to the renowned Guru Baba Muktananda during the 70's and early 80's Bud is also a well-known author, lecturer and teacher in the field of tantra yoga and meditation.

Printed in the USA
CPSIA information can be obtained
at www.ICGtesting.com
LVHW061513240424
778322LV00001B/1